SMALL
MISTAKES,
BIG
CONSEQUENCES

for
Interviews

*Hone your interviewing technique to present
your best self and land your dream job*

SMALL
MISTAKES,
BIG
CONSEQUENCES

for
Interviews

Discover
20 interview
skills you
need to
know

Anne Corley Baum
An Experienced Senior Executive
with a Witty Sense of Business Savvy

MOMOSA
PUBLISHING

© 2020 by Anne Corley Baum

Printed in the United States of America

Published in Hellertown, PA

Cover and interior design by Jennifer Giandomenico

Illustrations by Cielo Giandomenico and Jennifer Giandomenico

Library of Congress Control Number: 2020902176

ISBN 978-1-950459-00-1

2   4   6   8   10   9   7   5   3   1   paperback

This book is dedicated to my Aunt Libby,
who always helped me prepare for interviews,
and to Brad, Reed, Shay, and Lynd—love you!

Contents

Introduction

When I sat down to write the Small Mistakes, Big Consequences book series, my goal was to share common mistakes that prevent people from succeeding at their highest possible level. Every day when we interact with other people, we rarely think about our body language and behavior, yet these behaviors have a direct impact on how we are perceived by others.

First impressions are critically important in job interviews—when we have only a short time to make our best impression. During a job interview, small *mistakes* become *distractions* and cause the interviewer to focus on the mistake rather than on our capabilities and skills. In order to present your best self, it is critical to have the interviewer focus on the skills you bring to the table and how those skills are a match for the position for which the interview is being conducted.

Small Mistakes, Big Consequences for Interviews introduces 20 "business characters" that show up in interviews, often subconsciously, with the interviewee not even aware that they are happening. The goal of this book is to offer advice to both the interviewee and the interviewer to find the best person for the job, and the best job for the person!

When we meet someone new, we immediately make assumptions based upon how they look and behave. Perception *is* reality to the person with whom you are communicating. Beginning with the first phone call or email exchange you have with a company, you are making an impression. When you walk through the door for your interview, everyone from the receptionist, to the human resources coordinator, to the interviewer is forming their opinions of you. This guide is designed to help you present the best version of yourself and to help you get the job!

Enjoy!

> *Good is the enemy of great.*
> *—Jim Collins*

Small Mistake Number One

The Late Arriver

The Late Arriver shows up right at or after the scheduled appointment time. They often walk in with a casual, carefree air about them or rush in disheveled and stressed.

The Problem

Arriving late is disrespectful to the person with whom you are meeting. It sends the message that you don't care and that *your* time is more valuable and important to you than the job opportunity.

The Solution

Plan ahead and arrive early! Arrive at the location at least 30 minutes before the interview and enter the building at least 15 minutes before your scheduled appointment. Know where you are going, learn where to park, and understand how to find the office within the building. Make a practice run, see how traffic impacts the route and be well prepared.

If, despite your best efforts, you are delayed by traffic, weather, or some other circumstance, contact the company and let them know that you are on the way. Ask if they are still able to keep the appointment. Communication is key; don't assume they know where you are or what is happening.

For the Interviewer

Is There Potential?

Accidents, storms, and traffic happen. Try to gauge if the situation really caused a delay or if this person was late due to poor preparation. As long as the interviewee notified you of the delay and gave you a reasonable estimate of arrival time (and assuming you still have time in your schedule), give them a chance!

Know When It's Over

It is easy to determine if someone was late due to a real delay or if it was poor planning. If they are late and didn't notify you that they were delayed, or if they seem not to care, they probably aren't the right person for your position. Move on.

> *If I have made an appointment with you, I owe you punctuality, I have no right to throw away your time, if I do my own.*
> *—Richard Cecil*

Small Mistake Number Two

The Overconfident Overachiever

The Overconfident Overachiever is an arrogant braggart. They think they are smarter than the interviewer, and they are quick to share their expertise—whether asked to do so or not. Their inflated self-esteem is generally over the top and they tend to focus on how soon they can be promoted or move into the C-suite.

The Problem

Interviewers have a specific need when they post a job, and they aren't posting the job to advance *your* career. Though a good company cares for and invests in their employees, they do so to achieve their mission and vision, not necessarily yours. Overconfident Overachievers are a risky commodity because they aren't open to listening, learning, and being team players.

The Solution

Be the person a company will want to hire! Be enthusiastic about the company and not hypercritical. Be a great listener, and be willing to learn. Demonstrate how your skills and expertise meet the requirements of the job and will help the company achieve its goals. Show that you are teachable and also knowledgeable about the company's mission and vision. Be the person that a company hires for attitude and trains for skill.

For the Interviewer

Is There Potential?

In an effort to demonstrate that they are qualified for a job, some interviewees try too hard to explain their skills and expertise. Try asking questions to see what the person really knows and has experienced to gauge their real vs. overinflated skillset.

Know When It's Over

If you cannot redirect the person's focus and if they're fixated on telling you how great they are and how poorly your company is run, move on.

> *An arrogant person considers himself perfect. This is the chief harm of arrogance. It interferes with a person's main task in life—becoming a better person.*
> *—Leo Tolstoy*

Small Mistake Number Three

The Clueless Airhead

The Clueless Airhead doesn't take the interview seriously. They don't do their research, and they arrive at an interview with no knowledge of the job for which they are interviewing. They are ill prepared, and they present themselves as ditsy or spacey. They often use a lilty voice, giggle, look at the ceiling, or seem distracted.

The Problem

If an interviewee has not taken the time to prepare for an interview and cannot have an intelligent conversation about the role, the interviewer will likely remove the person from the candidate list. Competition is fierce and interviewers are looking for the WOW factor. They are quickly narrowing their list, and this behavior makes one an easy target for elimination.

The Solution

Do your research and be prepared! Understand the job for which you are interviewing. It is easier than ever to go online and research a company and the people with whom you will interview. As you research the company and interviewers, determine how your skillset matches with the job requirements and the company's culture. Determine what you have in common with the interviewers, and arrive well prepared.

For the Interviewer

Is There Potential?

If the interviewee has a good attitude, and you see potential, consider whether or not this person has the ability to learn. If they do, give them a shot!

Know When It's Over

If the person isn't taking the interview seriously, end the interview early and move on.

Small Mistake Number Four

The Messy Dresser

The Messy Dresser hasn't taken time to think about their appearance and how it impacts the first impression that they present. They may have rumpled hair, smeared or overdone makeup, wrinkled clothing, scuffed shoes, or unmanicured nails.

The Problem

When you look disheveled, you send a message that you don't care about yourself or the position for which you are interviewing. Whether it is fair or not, people make assumptions about you and your skills based upon your appearance. When you don't make a great first impression, it is much harder to recover and demonstrate your expertise and skills.

The Solution

Dress for success—Present your best self and look the part! When you look the part, the interviewer is imagining you in the role, and this great first impression sets the stage for a productive interview.

Do your research and check the company's website to see what the team is wearing in their photos. If they're wearing dark suits with white shirts and solid ties, dress more formally and wear something similar. Review the executive team's online profiles to get a feel for the dress code. If you are working with a recruiter, ask them for input on the attire for the interview. Invest in a good suit in a classic style that fits you well. Dark colors are best and the most versatile. Candidates always present well when dressed at the most professional level. Even when applying for an entry-level position, wear a suit. Look your best so interviewers see you at the highest possible level in their company and know you are taking the interview seriously.

Before the interview, test the fit of your clothing to make

sure it is comfortable. Sit, walk, and stand to be sure your skirt doesn't ride up too high or your trousers don't pull in awkward places. During the interview, it is important to concentrate on the conversation and the business at hand—not on adjusting your clothing.

Professionally dry clean and press your suits. Pay attention to your personal hygiene and grooming. Get a haircut. Wash your face. Wear subtle, not overdone makeup.

Smell clean, but don't go overboard with cologne or perfume. If you wear cologne or perfume, wear it lightly.

Before you leave for your interview, look at yourself in a mirror. Do you see a person that you would hire?

For the Interviewer

Is There Potential?

Get to know the person behind their messy appearance. Pull your attention away from how they dress and focus on their attitude and aptitude. Is there more to this person than their external appearance? If so, it is always possible to coach someone on their attire.

Know When It's Over

If you determine that an interviewee's disheveled attire and presentation matches the way they answer the questions and define their persona, move on.

Small Mistake Number Five

The Dining Dunce

The Dining Dunce doesn't demonstrate the basic dining etiquette. They use the wrong silverware, talk with their mouth

full, hold their silverware incorrectly, or order the most expensive item on the menu. They may drink too much during the meal and get drunk, slurp their food, smack their lips, chew with their mouth open, and treat the restaurant staff rudely.

The Problem

Poor table manners are distracting. During an interview over a meal, the focus should be on the conversation between you and the interviewer, not on poor table manners. The Dining Dunce is rude and uncouth, and this behavior makes others uncomfortable. Because many business meetings are conducted over meals, companies use interviews over meals to evaluate candidates. Manners say alot about the type of person you are, and poor manners or rude behavior are not attractive characteristics to interviewers.

The Solution

Learn the basics of dining etiquette! There is a wealth of information available online, an extensive array of books have been written, and classes are available to learn these easy skills. Most colleges and universities offer dining etiquette classes as do private consultants. Take time to learn the basics of this daily skill. It will pay off over your lifetime. Don't be intimidated by dining etiquette! Learn it and shine!

For the Interviewer

Is There Potential?

There is a fine line between someone who is rude and someone who just needs some education. Ask probing questions to ascertain where the interviewee falls on that line. Dining etiquette is a teachable skill. If the interviewee has simply had limited exposure to these skills, but has a wealth of knowledge for your company, give them a chance.

Know When It's Over

You can tell a lot about a person by observing how they treat others, especially the staff at a restaurant. Inherent rudeness is difficult to "teach away." If you sense that the interviewee is rude at their core, finish the meal, end the meeting, and move on.

> *Good manners are just a way of showing other people that we have respect for them.*
> *—Bill Kelly*

Small Mistake Number Six

The Text Talker,
Verbose Verbalizer,
or Casual Conversationalist

Dude, OMG, I cannot believe this kinda, sorta happened! Oh, and BTW our industrious palladrome is fastidious!

The Text Talker speaks in the same way that they text, using abbreviations such as LOL and OMG, instead of words. The Verbose Verbalizer attempts to sound intelligent and show off by using big words—often incorrectly. The Casual Conversationalist is too informal, using words like "hey," "dude," "kinda," and "sorta."

The Problem

All of these characters distract the interviewer and don't present the interviewee as intelligent, professional, or mature. Poor communication during an interview, when one should be at their very best, makes a person difficult to understand, and it also impacts the overall impression that one is making. Communication is key to most businesses. Failure to demonstrate your ability to communicate well at the time when you should be presenting the best version of yourself, will generally result in not receiving a call back or job offer.

The Solution

Speak professionally, clearly, and concisely, using correct grammar! Don't overuse abbreviations, jargon, or long complicated words. Speak clearly and concisely, take your time, present well thought-out answers.

For Interviewers

Is There Potential?

Most people who speak this way don't realize they are doing so. It's a habit they have developed, and it can be changed. Try to listen beyond the abbreviations, jargon, and big words to assess their depth of knowledge and skill. They may have potential and can be coached on language skills.

Know When It's Over

If you can't understand anything the interviewee is saying, even if you are doing your best to listen beyond the abbreviations or big words, close the interview and move on.

> *The single biggest problem in communication is the illusion that it has taken place.*
> *—George Bernard Shaw*

Small Mistake Number Seven

The Interrupter

The Interrupter is always interjecting their thoughts and opinions while others are still speaking. They don't let people finish sentences and jump in to answer before they've even heard the full question.

The Problem

People don't like to be interrupted. It's rude, and it makes others feel that their thoughts and ideas are not being heard or that they are unimportant. When one answers a question before it's completely asked, they run the risk of answering the wrong question and find themselves in an awkward position.

The Solution

Be a great listener! Let people finish their sentences, and formulate your answer so you get it right. People sometimes interrupt because they are passionate or excited about a topic or they simply get carried away. Control your excitement, listen to what is being said, and interject your thoughts, when the other person finishes or pauses (in a calm, collected manner).

For Interviewers

Is There Potential?

If you sense the interruptions are driven by excitement and passion, there may be potential with the candidate. Steer the person back to the topic at hand and listen to their comments and ideas.

Know When It's Over

If you can't successfully steer the person back to the conversation, if they are not answering your questions, or if you sense the interruptions are driven by rudeness, move on.

Small Mistake Number Eight

The Gawker

The Gawker is brash and flirty. They stare at the body parts of others or have inappropriate eye contact. They may use sexual innuendo, make inappropriate comments or behave in an aggressively suave manner.

The Problem

There is no place in an interview for anything sexual, not even a hint of it. It is inappropriate and sends the wrong message about who you are. An interview is not the time or place for flirting or acknowledging attraction. Some people think they are being charming; however, it is off-putting and very unprofessional to behave in this manner.

The Solution

Be professional! Avoid jokes or raucous humor that could be misunderstood. Stay away from comments that are racial, political, religious, or sexual. There is no reason to offend the interviewer by making off color comments or hitting on them.

For Interviewers

Is There Potential?

Some people don't realize that these comments are inappropriate and unprofessional. If you sense that they are coachable and have solid underlying skills that, with coaching, could be corrected, consider them for the role.

Know When It's Over

Poor behavior of this type is hard to "unteach." If the person's entire interview is punctuated by inappropriate comments, or if they say things unconsciously that they don't even realize are inappropriate, move on.

Small Mistake
Number Nine

The Nodder

The Nodder constantly nods their head, whether they actually agree with the speaker or not. Sometimes they will add words like: yes, uh huh, hmm.

The Problem

When a person nods, their body language is signaling agreement even though they may simply be listening. If a person is nodding because they are listening, and then says something to disagree, the receiver feels a disconnect and wonders why the Nodder changed their mind! A disconnect between the message your body language sends and the words you use can make one appear to be dishonest or false.

The Solution

Be mindful of your body language and facial expressions! Pay attention to your body language and match it to the words you use. Do you nod your head regularly as a way of listening? This exercise can help: While you are on the phone, watch yourself in a mirror and observe your body language and facial expressions. Are you shaking your head no but saying yes? Are you saying you agree while scowling or shaking your head no? People perceive body language and facial expressions first, and well before they actually listen to what you have to say. Learn how to match your body language and facial expressions to your intended message and the words you use. It will make a tremendous difference in the effectiveness of your communication.

For Interviewers

Is There Potential?

This characteristic is rarely a deal breaker. Nodding is a habit, and habits can be broken. Don't assume that someone is agreeing just because they are nodding. Try to encourage the person to tell you what they think, without making assumptions based upon the body language you observe.

Know When It's Over

If you sense that the person is not authentic or is dishonest, don't move them forward. If you sense this is a "yes"-person, someone who agrees with everything, that may be a deal-breaker, move on.

> *Body language and tone of voice—not words— are our most powerful assessment tools. —Christopher Voss*

Small Mistake
Number Ten

The Downlooker

The Downlooker doesn't make eye contact and prefers to look at the floor, the table, and anything that isn't a person. They are often shy or reserved and are uncomfortable looking others in the eye.

The Problem

When you don't make eye contact, it sends a message of shyness, hesitance, and lack of confidence. It can also send a message that you are not trustworthy or that you are not confident in your abilities.

The Solution

Make eye contact! Eye contact demonstrates confidence, and it shows people that you are listening. When you look someone in the eye, it helps you to read the other person's facial expressions and interpret how they are responding to your comments.

Handy tip: If it's difficult to make eye contact, look at the space right between the eyes of the person (the safe zone). It will appear that you are looking them directly in the eye.

For Interviewers

Is There Potential?

Don't completely write a person off if they aren't making eye contact. They may just be shy or lack confidence. If you see potential, eye contact can be taught.

Know When It's Over

If you sense the reason for the lack of eye contact is that the person isn't trustworthy, try asking probing questions to determine if the person is shifty or shy. If they're not trustworthy, move on.

Small Mistake
Number Eleven

The Nervous Nellie

The Nervous Nellie is timid and anxious. They tend to have distracting habits like tapping their pens on the table, shaking

the change in their pockets, or speaking very quickly. They are on anxiety overload. Nervousness exudes from their bodies. Their faces may be flushed, and they may even be sweating excessively.

The Problem

It's distracting and hard to pay attention when someone is visibly nervous. Anxiety is contagious. It can make the interviewer feel uncomfortable and distract them from the talents you possess.

The Solution

Believe in yourself! Present yourself as calm and collected—even if you don't completely feel it. Combat anxiety with confidence. If you're anxious or nervous, practice calming techniques prior to the interview. Play your psych-up song/playlist before you go into the interview. Give yourself a pep talk or talk with friends who support and encourage you. Practice yoga or deep breathing.

Learn your nervous habits. They are often subconscious, so ask a friend to observe you and share what they observe. Once you are aware, develop strategies to combat these behaviors. For example, if you twirl your hair, wear it up or pulled back. If you jingle coins or keys in your pocket, empty your pockets. If you click pens, don't hold a pen in your hand or use one that doesn't have a clicker. If you tend to sweat, take a shower and wear excellent antiperspirant.

Remember: You may feel nervous, but others don't necessarily perceive your nerves. Talk yourself through the fear and keep going!

For Interviewers

Is There Potential?

If the interviewee is nervous, try to put them at ease. Make them feel comfortable and listen to what the interviewee is saying. Give them the benefit of the doubt. The nerves may be interview related.

Know When It's Over

If the person cannot have a conversation beyond their nervousness, despite your best efforts to put them at ease, it's time to move on.

Know your value. Confidence breeds success. Act like the person you want to become, and people will start seeing you as that person.
—Mark M. Ford

Small Mistake Number Twelve

The Judgmental Jerk

The Judgmental Jerk is hypercritical and comes into the interview telling you all of the ways that your company needs to improve. They judge the company and tell you how bad things are—without offering productive solutions.

The Problem

Judgmental Jerks present themselves as arrogant, narrow-minded, and presumptuous. This is offensive to the interviewer and puts them in a defensive position. Ironically, Judgmental Jerks often lack confidence, but they present themselves as very aggressive and negative.

The Solution

Don't judge! Present ideas in a productive manner. Offer productive solutions for how you would help the organization find success through the role for which you are interviewing. Ask probing questions and understand the frame of reference of the interviewer.

For Interviewers

Is There Potential?

Sometimes, someone who appears to be judgmental may just be forward in expressing their opinions. Try to determine if they have good ideas. You might learn something that can be of value to your organization.

Know When It's Over

If you determine that this is an arrogant, pushy person who's unwilling to listen, move on.

Small Mistake Number Thirteen

The Personal Shopper

The Personal Shopper only cares about what the company can do for them. They are shopping for benefits, perks, and

anything that makes their life easier. They tend to focus on benefits, vacation days, and other benefits during the interview. They are relentlessly focused on what the company can do for them—instead of what they can do for the company.

The Problem

When a company posts a job, they are posting it because they have a business need. They are not posting it to sell their benefits packages. They need a resource, a skillset, and a set of talents. Companies provide benefits to hire great employees, but when you focus on what the company can do for you, versus what you can do for the company, you send the message that you care about yourself more than their business.

The Solution

Focus on what *you* can do for the company! Position yourself to match the skills the company is seeking. Once you are offered the job, you can negotiate benefits. If the benefits don't match your needs, you don't have to take the job. Benefits are a secondary discussion and are part of the offer negotiations, not part of the interview.

For Interviewers

Is There Potential?

Some people worry about benefits and others are naïve. Ask questions in a way that helps the interviewee focus their skillset so you can determine if they are qualified and have the skills for which you are hiring.

Know When It's Over

If you can't direct the interviewee to answer questions pertaining to the job and they show no interest in your company or the position, move on.

Small Mistake Number Fourteen

The Gushy Complimenter

The Gushy Complimenter goes over the top with compliments. Their free flow of compliments often strings together phrases like, "I love your office! It's awesome! What a great company! You're amazing! Don't you just LOVE working here?"

The Problem

Too many compliments, especially delivered in a long stream of words with no break, seem insincere and present the candidate as nervous or shallow. When you overdo compliments, people stop believing you. Too many compliments may be perceived as unprofessional. Also, if you offer compliments about a person's appearance, especially if the person is of the opposite gender, it may be misinterpreted as flirty or overly familiar.

The Solution

Focus on your skills and the job! Learn everything possible about the job and the necessary qualifications, ask good questions, be prepared, and focus on the role. Listen to what the interviewer is saying and prepare good answers. Set yourself up as the right person for the job. Don't get distracted talking about light-hearted, fluffy topics. Present yourself as someone who is sincerely interested in the job.

For Interviewers

Is There Potential?

Some people are really excited and genuinely love the company. They might have a true admiration for you and are excited about the job. Don't misinterpret real excitement for insincerity; give them a chance. Try not to be distracted by light-hearted compliments. Accept the compliment by saying thank you and move the conversation on to the more important, substantive questions.

Know When It's Over

If you find, after asking substantive questions, that the candidate doesn't have any depth to them or they really don't have the skills you are seeking, move on.

> *To practice five things under all circumstances constitutes perfect virtue; these five are gravity, generosity of soul, sincerity, earnestness, and kindness.*
> *—Confucius*

Small Mistake Number Fifteen

The Name Dropper

The Name Dropper constantly mentions the names of people that they think are important in order to demonstrate their

value. They want the interviewer to think that they know all of the important people to demonstrate that they are important. They appear to show off by throwing around names of people they think are important in an effort to impress the interviewer.

The Problem

Name droppers are perceived as arrogant, snobbish, or shallow. When someone is constantly name dropping, it takes away from who *they* are and what they have to offer. It also presents the person as if they think they are better than others or they are trying to show off. Dropping names with whom the interviewer is unfamiliar can make the interviewer uncomfortable or feel disconnected. If you drop a name of a person about whom the interviewer has a poor opinion, it may reflect poorly upon you. Your reputation is impacted by the company that you keep!

The Solution

Sell yourself on *your* merits—who *you* are and what *you* bring to the role. It's not necessary to use someone else's reputation to encourage a company to hire you. If you know people, and that benefits the organization, that's great. There is no reason to share that information to prove your value. The company is hiring you for *your* skills and talents, not the people you know. Make sure you let your value shine through.

For Interviewers

Is There Potential?

Ask yourself if the Name Dropper actually *knows* the people they are mentioning and if those relationships are advantageous to your company. Sometimes, it does matter who you know. Determine if the interviewee really does have these connections and how that person might bring value to the job through these connections. There may be potential in these relationships, if they are real.

Know When It's Over

Some people are excessive Name Droppers. All they do is talk about people they know. If the Name Dropper also gossips or if the people they mention are of ill repute, think twice about that person and move on.

A man is known by the company he keeps.
—Aesop

Small Mistake Number Sixteen

The Complicated Scheduler

Complicated Schedulers make it difficult to schedule the interview, or they reschedule excessively.

The Problem

This appointment is not about you and your schedule; it's about adapting your schedule to meet the options the company has available. Complicated Schedulers appear inflexible—even disorganized.

If you make scheduling too hard, the company may not give you another option, and the opportunity could be lost.

The Solution

Prioritize interviews. Go out of your way to reschedule your personal appointments and find a way to accomodate the interviewer. Show them that the interview is a priority—this sends a positive message about you and your commitment to the role.

If something completely unavoidable happens at the last minute (e.g., burst appendix), contact the company immediately to explain and reschedule.

For Interviewers

Is There Potential?

Though it is frustrating to work with the Complicated Scheduler, consider that the person may be struggling with their job, family, or school schedule, particularly if it's early in their career or they have young children. Don't automatically rule them out if they have scheduling problems. Give them the benefit of the doubt. For example, a single parent, trying to move up in the world, whose babysitter falls through at the last minute, deserves a second chance.

Know When It's Over

Use the "three strikes you're out" rule. If an interviewee is rescheduling for a third time, move on.

> *Your word is your honor.*
> *If you say you're going to do something,*
> *then you need to do it.*
> *—Joyce Meyer*

Small Mistake Number Seventeen

The Excuser

The Excuser doesn't take ownership or responsibility for anything. They don't own their problems or mistakes. There is always an excuse and it's always someone else's fault.

There is a big difference between offering an excuse versus an explanation. An excuse places the blame on someone or something else. (I'm late because my mom didn't wake me up.) An explanation gives the context of why something happened, while taking responsibility for the result that occurred. (I set

That assistant gave me the wrong floor and didn't warn me about the security delay!

my alarm, and I'm late because the power went out overnight. It's no excuse, but I wanted you to know what happened. It will never happen again.)

The Problem

Excusers are unreliable. When someone doesn't own their mistakes and blames others, they usually are not team players. They are always looking for someone at which they can point a finger.

The Solution

Take ownership, be responsible. Stand up and lead your own life with pride and confidence. Don't look to place blame about your situation on others, own your mistakes and learn from them!

For Interviewers

Is There Potential?

Listen carefully to what the person is saying. Are they making excuses and blaming other people, situations, or things? Is this a legitimate explanation and are they still owning it? If they're owning it, there's an opportunity, give them a chance.

Know When It's Over

If you listen and the interviewee is pointing fingers, placing blame, and not taking ownership, it could be a really poor decision to bring them onto the team. Not only is an Excuser a poor team player, they can disrupt your entire culture—move on.

Small Mistake Number Eighteen

The Choosey Assumer

The Choosey Assumer rules out an interview or even an entire company based on assumptions. They come up with a list of reasons why the job or company isn't a good fit for them before they even apply for the job.

The Problem

When you make assumptions, you are missing an opportunity to learn the truth. When you assume, you are guaranteeing that what *you* think is true and not taking a chance to learn the truth about the opportunity.

The Solution

Take a risk; go to the interview. The only way you can know if your assumptions are correct is by verifying them yourself. Ask good questions and search for the real story. You may be pleasantly surprised and find the perfect job!

For Interviewers

Is There Potential?

Often, the Choosey Assumer doesn't even make it to the interview! If they show up and are making a lot of assumptions, see how well they respond when you tell them the real story. People don't often realize that they are basing something on assumption rather than fact. Clarify the facts for them and see how they respond.

Know When It's Over

Since the Choosey Assumer doesn't even make it to the interview, you don't have to worry: It's already over.

Small Mistake Number Nineteen

The Gum Chomper

The Gum Chomper comes to the interview with gum, candy, or cough drops in their mouth. They chew with an open mouth, blow bubbles, or make popping sounds.

The Problem

Having anything in your mouth, eating candy, or bringing your own coffee into the room is distracting, too casual, and takes attention away from what you're saying.

The Solution

Don't have anything in your mouth. Make sure you don't have anything to prevent you from speaking clearly and professionally. Whether it's a retainer or a piece of gum, remove it! Let the interviewer focus on you and the words you use. If you have a cough, take cough medicine before the interview. Don't take the risk of anything in your mouth flying out, causing you to choke, or getting in the way of your words.

For Interviewers

Is There Potential?

Sure! You can teach someone this easy lesson. They might not be aware of the distraction or may have a cough or cold. Try not to judge them for it and give them a chance.

Know When It's Over

If they are rude or unpolished, blowing bubbles, or chomping on their gum, and they don't have anything to offer, move on.

Small Mistake Number Twenty

The Heinous Handshaker

The Heinous Handshaker delivers a wimpy or bone-crushing handshake. They either over- or under-do the handshake and leave the other person feeling awkward.

The Problem

Your handshake sends a subliminal message of who you are. A poor handshake sends the message that you're unprofessional, too aggressive or too weak.

Note

During times when personal or community health is at risk, handshaking may not be safe or appropriate. It is still important to greet others professionally. Make great eye contact as soon as possible, stop at a safe distance, smile, and acknowledge the awkwardness of the situation. State that you are not shaking hands at this time due health and safety concerns. Introduce yourself, smile, nod, and move on to the business at hand. When you take charge of the situation, it puts the other person at ease, demonstrates confidence, and helps what could be an uncomfortable situation move forward smoothly.

Shaking hands for too long leaves you holding hands and is awkward. A bone-crushing handshake sends a message of aggressiveness, while a soft handshake sends a message of weakness.

Hugging someone instead of shaking hands on a first meeting is too familiar, and it makes the other person feel uncomfortable.

The Solution

Offer your hand in a firm handshake as soon as you meet someone. Learn and practice your handshake. Look them in the eye and smile! It sends an important message about who you are. Make it great!

For Interviewers

Is There Potential?

Get to know the person behind the handshake. Many people haven't had the opportunity to learn how to correctly execute a handshake. This is a teachable skill. If this is your only issue, give them a chance.

Know When It's Over

Though this is a teachable skill, it does make an impression. If the person's interview solidifies the perception established by the handshake, move on.

You did it! Interview complete! Now what? Before you go, thank the interviewer for the interview. Understand the next steps and send them a thank you note!

Strategies for Success

Quick Tips to Help Keep You on Track

1) Plan ahead and arrive early.
2) Be the person a company will want to hire.
3) Do your research and be prepared.
4) Dress for success. Present your best self and look the part.
5) Learn the basics of dining etiquette.
6) Speak professionally, clearly, and concisely, using correct grammar.
7) Be a great listener.
8) Stay professional.
9) Be mindful of your body language and facial expressions.
10) Make eye contact.
11) Believe in yourself.
12) Don't judge.
13) Focus on what *you* can do for the company.
14) Focus the conversation on the job and your skills.
15) Sell yourself on *your* merits—who *you* are and what *you* bring to the role.
16) Prioritize interviews.
17) Take ownership; be responsible.
18) Take a risk; go to the interview.
19) Don't have anything in your mouth when speaking.
20) If handshaking is safe and appropriate, offer your hand in a firm handshake as soon as you meet someone.

About the Author

Anne Corley Baum is the Lehigh Valley executive and vice president, distribution channels and labor relations for Capital BlueCross. She is the senior leader in the Capital BlueCross Lehigh Valley office. Anne leads the network of more than 5,500 producers, and is also responsible for the plan's organized labor customers.

Since joining the company in January 2010, Anne has been involved with strategic planning, operations, partnership development, community relations, corporate giving, sales, and account management throughout Capital BlueCross' eastern service area.

She is also the owner of Vision Accomplished, a firm dedicated to leadership and culture. Anne is active in the community and has served in leadership roles with many boards and executive committees.

She has received a number of awards, including Best 50 Women in PA Business, the Lehigh Valley SUITS award, Leukemia and Lymphoma Society Woman of the Year, the Girl Scout's Take the Lead Award, the ATHENA International Award, Woman of Influence from Lehigh Valley Business, the Golden Laurel Award from the YWCA and volunteer of the year by both the United Way and the Greater Lehigh Valley Chamber of Commerce.

A native of Glenview, IL, Anne holds a BS in Biology from the University of Illinois, Champaign-Urbana, IL, and an MS in Health Systems Management from Rush University, Chicago, IL. She is certified by the Protocol School of Washington as a protocol and etiquette consultant.

She is a proud mother of two wonderful children and is married to her high school sweetheart.

Acknowledgments

Thank you to Jennifer Bright and the team at Momosa Publishing for helping make this book a reality; to Janet Appel, Jennifer Abernethy, and Sara Wotherspoon for getting the word out and telling the story so well. As always, thanks to Jessie Seneca for the "push" and to Shelley, Drea, Tony, Mom, Brad, Reed, and Shay for your friendship, love, and support!

Coming soon from Vision Accomplished and Momosa Publishing:

Small Mistakes, Big Consequences for Conference Calls
Small Mistakes, Big Consequences for College

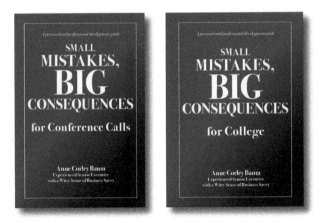